The best of
Andorra

© Copyright :EDICIONS A. CAMPAÑÀ
C/ Alcalde de Móstoles, 19. 08025 BARCELONA
Tel: (93) 456 43 36 - Fax: (93) 450 18 89
Fotografías: Antoni Campañà Capella
Coordinació: Margarita Campañà
Text: Joana Viusà i Galí
Fotocomposició: JEBA SA. C/ Marina 221,baixos 0802BARCELONA
I.S.B.N. 84-86294-57-6
Dep. Legal: B-23.108-98
Printed: FUTURGRAFIC S.C.C.L.

Distribució: Comercial FORN, S.L.
Casa de la roca, Pont de Molleres. Meritxell - CANILLO
Tel:: 85 19 02 - Fax: 85 17 44 - Principat d'Andorra

Altres fotografs: AVIOTEC, Pags: 2,14,15,2527,29,74. Luciano Tomé, pags: 10,16,21,92,93,94,95. UPT Canillo, pags: 12,13,16,66,92,93,94,95. Art Creatiu, pags: 30,32. Enric Madrenas, pag: 31. Carlos Jorge, pag: 32. Gonzalo Azumendi, pag: 80. AGE Fotostock, pag: 82. Cedidas per Rosa Albert, pag: 91.

The best of
Andorra

Andorra is a small independent state, 488 Km2, deep in the Pyrenee mountains. The official language is Catalan but French and Spanish are also spoken. The inhabitants are a mixture of 130 different nationalities, among which Andorran is the second in number 13,000 citizens, first is Spanish (28,656) followed by Portugese (6,886), French (4,352) and the Anglophonic community (approx.1,500 British, Americans and Australians).

The Principality of Andorra is the second highest country in Europe, after Switzerland - and it is worth escaping from the commercial centre, to wander among its beautiful lakes, fresh rivers and high mountains, both in winter and summer. A countryside where you can find 45 medieval Romanic churches as well as many medieval bridges.

There are thirtyfive km from the Spanish border to the French frontier. These can be covered in 45 minutes, from 829 metres height at the Spanish-Andorran border to 2,440m. in Pas de la Casa.

There are various roads from Barcelona: it takes 3 hours to cover the 225km. Madrid and Paris are, more or less, the same distance from Andorra: approx. 850km. The nearest airports are Tolosa del Llenguadoc (200km) and Barcelona. Currently the Andorran and Catalan governments are negociating the reopening of Seu d'Urgell airport, closed in 1983.

The survivial of such a small country, between the two great States of France and Spain, throughout the centuries can only be explained by its difficult access and for the tenacity of its inhabitants. The statutes are inherited directly from the feudal era.

On the previous page a view of Angonella lake. Top left Andorra al Vella and the Andorran flag. Above the Valira d'Orient river with Montmalús in the background.

ANDORRA

FRANÇA

Estany
de
Cabana
Sorda

Estanys
de
Juclar

Vall d'Incles

EL TARTER

Estany
d'Incles

SOLDEU

Sant Joan de
Caselles

NILLO

ntuari de
eritxell

PAS DE LA CASA

Aduana

Pic dels Alts
del Cubíl
2.833 m.

rtals d'Encamp
ters

Pic dels
Pessons
2.858 m.

Port d'Envalira

FRANÇA

GRAU ROIG

Estany dels
Pessons

Estany de
Montmalús

Estany Forcat

ny de
afita

Estació d'esquí alpí

Estació d'esquí de fons

Above left, the hall of the general Consell of the Valls d'Andorra. On the right, the kitchen of the Casa de la Vall. Below left, the hall of lost steps of the Consell General and antique dinning room of the Casa de la Vall.

Its inaccessability is due to the natural mountain fortress which surrounds it, longer than 110km, 108km. of which are between 2,000 metres and approx. 3,000 metres high. The summits form a circle, the highest, Comapedrosa is 2,942 metres. The Valira river has its source in this circle, later mixing with the waters of the Segre river in Seu d'Urgell.

THE PARIATGES, FOUNDING DOCUMENTS OF THE CO-PRINCIPALITY

Apart from an Andosin village mentioned by the Greek Polibi in the description of Hanibal's crossing of the Pyrenees, the Valley of Andorra was first heard of in 839, in the Consecration of the Cathedral of Seu d'Urgell, capital of the "Comtat d'Urgell", integrated in the "Marca Hispanica" created by Charlemagne.

Above a retrospective photo of the Consell General and the Co-Principat d'Andorra. Below on the left the commemorative Monument to the Pariatges and Andorran Constitution, in the gardens of the Casa de la Vall, on the right the coat of arms of the Principality, 1763, above the door of the Casa de la Vall.

A marvellous view Valira d'Orient and Incles rivers where they join.

During the XII Century, the Count of Urgell, Ermengol VI gave Andorra to Bishop Pere Berenguer who, to protect his domains from the neighbouring barons, conceded his Andorran territories to one of them, Senyor de Caboet, unfortunately for the "Iglesia d' Urgell" they soon passed, by marriage, to the powerful Count of Foix, protector of the Cathers. Count Roger Bernat de Foix, did not accept vassalage and made war on the Bishop.

The bloody battles ended with the "Pariatges", the first was signed in 1278, and the second in 1288 by the competitors and Pere II of Catalonia and III of Aragon, and were endorsed by papal bull by Pope Marti IV:The "Pariatges" consegrated the control of the Co-principality of the Valls d'Andorra between the Bishop and the Count of Foix, which has lasted until our times.

However, while one of the Co-princes has always been the Bishop of Urgell, on the side of the Count of Foix it passed from Count, to King, to Emperor and, finally to the President of the French Republic.

The Valira river by El Serrat. Below Nou lake.

A spectacular view of the Moles horse tail waterfall in Canillo, an adequate place for picnics.

In 1607, after being crowned King of France, the Co-prince of Foix and King of Navarra, Enric IV, gave his rights over Andorra to the Crown, until 1793 when the French revolution rejected the feudal tribute paid by the Andorrans (the QÄestia).

In 1806 the Andorans, conscious that if they depended only on the Bishop they would soon be absorbed by Spain, went to Paris and convinced Napoleon to re-establish the title of Co-Prince of Andorra.

A beautiful perspective of the numerous curves on the road to Envalira Pass in the middle of winter. All the Vall d'Envalira is visible with the ski slopes of Soldeu el Tarter on the left.

However, only 6 years later, on annexing Catalonia to his empire, Napoleon specified that it included the Vall d'Andorra. This time the Andorran leaders did not go to Paris to negociate, they stopped in Perpinya, with the result that the Prefect of the Department of the Eastern Pyrenees "forgot" to include the Vall d'Andorra in his department.

The last scare for Andorra was in November 1943, when the Wermacht, which had occupied the south of France neared the Port d'Envalira. This time the episcopal co-prince obtained help from General Franco in Spain, who stopped the German army's advance.

Throughout its history Andorra has been self-governed: first there was the "Parroquia". Later, in 1419, the Co-princes conceded the creation of the "Consell de la Terra", embreo of a parlimentary assembly, representing the 6 territories which then existed. With the Nova Reforma in 1866 the name was changed to Consell General de las Valls.

Winter view of Juclar lake
Mountain sports, climbing the via Ferrata, on the Roc del Quer in Canillo.

More than a century later, in 1981 the co-princes agreed to a second institutional reform and decreed an executive Consell, separate from the parlimentary assembly. But parlimentary representation has always been territorial and it was not until the Constitution in 1993 that there could be a mixed parliament which would introduce national representation.

Currently each of the 7 "Parroquies" elect 2 candidates from their own "Parroquia" instead of 4, and 2 other national representatives. Therefore, the "Consell General" is formed by 14 deputies, territorial representatives and 14 national representatives, elected by the country, 10,836 electorate.

The 28 members of the "Consell general" meet in the "sala d'Actas", on the first floor of the "Casa de la Vall", in Andorra la Vella. From the XII Century until 1978 the parchments of the founding documents and the different "Privilegis" granted to the Andorrans by the neighbouring monarchs were kept in the venerable "Armari de les 6 Claus".(Cupboard of six keys).

"La Casa de la Vall" is a magnificent ancestral seat from the XVI Century and dominates the Valira valley, from the high

mount where the house and capital of the country were constructed. It is seen as a museum of traditions: it still conserves the antique kitchen with its utensils and the bedrooms with the poor bunks where the councellors of the "Paroquies" often had to sleep as they could not return home because of the snow.

On the left Valira d'Orient river near Arinsal and below the frozen mountain lake of Comapedrosa, below the highest peak of Andorra (2,946m) of the same name. Above a beautiful aerial view of Juclar lake.

Until recently the lower floor, built inside the rock was the detention centre where they kept petty criminals, the ones who had been sentenced had to choose between French or Spanish prisons. It had its own restaurant. There is now a completely new prison in La Comella on the other side of the river and the prison officers no longer have to pass in front of the church of Sant Esteve where the criminals could hide.

The Tribunal de Corts where the trials are held is on the ground floor of the Casa de La Vall.

The first Penal Code of Andorra was made immediately after the institutional

Juclar lake above and Tristaina lake below

A beautiful bronze monument called "the dance" dedicated to the sardana, a typical dance in Andorra and Catalonia,in the gardens of the Casa de la Vall.

change. Until recently the law was ruled by Usos i Costums, the Dret Romá, the Dret Catalá and Spanish or French laws were referred to to judge more modern crimes.

On March 14th, 1993 for the first time in their history Andorrans adopted a modern Consitution and July 28th of the same year Andorra became the 184 State member of the UN.

Andorra still has two Co-princes, the President of the French Republic and the Bishop of the Seu d'Urgell, but they do not intervene in the affairs of the Country as they did previous to 1993, when they still had an almost Feudal tie with their subjects. Nowadays, they are limited to act as Andorran Heads of State.

Even with the constitutional change the medieval origin of Andorra is conserved with the territorial division in Parroquies, governed by Comuns. During 7 centuries there were 6 Parroquies. From 1978, there are 7, due to a

Graphic testament of Andorra la Vella at the beginning of the century. Below a detail of the monument to the sardana "la Dansa".

there were 6 Parroquies. From 1978, there are 7, due to a decree by the Co-princes which divided the Parroqia of Andorra la Vell, creating Escaldes-Engordany. Half of the population of the country live in these two territories. However, these territories are still divided according to historic protocol which, in previous centuries corresponded to the number of inhabitants, heads of cattle and wealth.

The first Parroquia is Canillo, then Encamp, Ordino, La Massana, Andorra la Vella, Sant Juliá de Loria and the most recent Parroquia, Escaldes-Engordany.

The town of Santa Coloma is an integral part of the Parroquia of Andorra la Vella, even though it is some kilometres below the capital and its name appears in the Act of consecration

Entrance to the Casa de la Vall by the gardens which surround it and the dorran flag, symbol of this country.

pre-Romanic church with its round bell tower - is testimony to its importance in the Middle Ages. This tower - a rare example of circular Romanic towers- is 18 metres high with Llombard arcatures. The horseshoe arch in the square nave is Visigoth and the arch which leads to the apse is Mozarabic.

A TAX-FREE COUNTRY

The Andorrans not only know how to avoid invaders. Their talent as negociator - taking advantage of the differences between the two Co-princes- won them fiscal priviledges, which, even though they may have promoted the smuggling of tobacco,

The Romanic church of Santa Coloma, unique example of Pyreneic Romanesque.

have made an emormous commercial growth possible since the 50's.

Today, the Principality of Andorra is a member of the UN, UNESCO and the European Counsel, however, it is not a member of the European Unity. For a simple reason: Andorra does not wish to lose its special fiscal status which does not have a direct tax. The inhabitants of Andorra pay only a small family contribution called Foc i Lloc which each communal administration charges. From 1994, the 6 banks contributed 3,200 million pesetas to the public treasury.

A 90% of the State budget (27,000 million pesetas) comes from taxes on merchandise charged the Andorran Customs at both frontiers. As these taxes are not more than 15% of the value of the goods, this makes the products more attractive, whether designer brands or general luxury items : the more expensive they are and the more tax they pay in their countries of origen the greater the difference in price on the Andorran market.

The country became known after the Spanish and European wars, due to the modern consumer products from France,

Above. Sant Viçens castle, a detail of the bell tower and the cylindric tower 17.5 m. in height. On the left the entrance to Santa Coloma church and a detail of the church gardens. Below the Romanic bridge, Margineda.

Above, Sant Esteve d'Andorra la Vella church. Above right a detail of the second door of Sant Esteve church, in centre a sculpture dedicated to the co-prince Bishop Benlloc,in front of the church. Below a view of the Passeig of the Plaça del Poble.

Sant Esteve church from the Plaça del Poble, in Andorra la Vella.

which the Spanish citizens began to buy. Stainless Steel pans, Duralex glass and nylon were the first products offered on the Andorran market.

A Catalan writer, Esteve Albert, contributed to attracting the first coaches of tourists, by organizing a Live Nativity Play in Engordany, where all the village participated, while shops began to mushroom along the Meritxell Avenue of Andorra la Vella and Carlemany of Escaldes-Engordany.

On the decrease of the fiscal difference between France and Spain, consequence of the unification of taxes on products from members of the European Unity, Andorra tried to diversify its appeal, which does not now centre exclusively on its long commercial avenue.

During the last 20 years, the number of winter tourists has grown more than the commercial ones, in benefit of the ski resorts and luxury shops.

Above, the "Mirador" of Andorra la Vella and below, a view of Central Park.

The upper photo is a general aerial view of Andorra la Vella and in the background, Escaldes Engordany. The two lower photos are the water area of Central Park.

The upper photo is a view of the Romanic church of Sant Miquel d'Engolasters.
On the right a view, in close up Sant Miquel d'Engolaster above Escaldes Engordany and in the background Andorra la Vella.

ESCALDES-ENGORDANY.

The Parroquia of Escaldes-Engordany created in 1978, is the newest of the 7 Parroquies. It is the paradigm of growth in commerce and demographic explosion as well as being the most urban. The asphalt of its long Carlemany Avenue grew from the potatoe and tobacco fields which, decades ago separated the old town of Escaldes-Engordany from the capital a kilometre away.

At weekends or holidays, Authentic rivers of tourists flow up and down this road, untiringly comparing prices. Some years ago the cheap whiskys and cheeses attracted coaches full of one day shoppers. The number of supermarkets to the square metre is probably the highest in Europe. But, nowadays, there is a proliferation of shops with Hi-fi equipment and cameras as well as fashion and perfume shops selling exclusive brands. This shows a radical change in the type of tourist along the longest commercial avenue in the Pyrenees.

On the left, a view of the main facade of the church of Sant Pere Mártir of Escaldes Engordany.

On the left the Romanic bridge in Escaldes Engordany.
Below a small park above the fountains of thermal waters
On the right page, the "Roc del Metge", in the same
place as the source of thermal waters in Escaldes
Engordany

General aerial view of Escaldes Engordany and in the background, Andorra la Vella, where we can we see the configuration of the valley

The name Escaldes (warm waters) clearly refers to the hot mineral waters (75%, the hotest in Europe) which spring from different sources on the banks of the Valira d'orient river.

Such warm water made for an intense activity of members of the wool trade and wool combers, a flourishing activity in the XVII century which finished at the end of the XIX century. The hot water in old houses in the town centre has always come from these springs and until the 80's

Two nocturnal aspects of the ludic spa Caldea in Escaldes Engordany

An exterior view of the ludic spa Caldea where we the glass structure.

there was still a communal wash house. The Carlemany and Roc Blanc hotels are well known for their spa waters. When the cold winter freezes hands, it is very agreeable to approach these boiling waters in the three public fountains in Sant Anna square,

Escoles Avenue and on the other side of the street, the leafy monument on the top of a hill crowned by a smoking tower.

At the end of the 80's the Comu d'Escaldes-Engordany decided to exploit this natural richness, sinking wells to get more water flow. The result is the magnificent ludic-sport complex of Caldea, which offers hydro-massage, fitness, saunas or swimming in warm rivers in natural scenery in the open air. The pyramidical,

In the upper photo, Caldea and the surrounding gardens.
Below, an interior view of the installations of the ludic spa Caldea.

Two aspects of the installations of the ludic spa Caldea, one of Andorra's main attractions.

transparent superstructure of the building is part of the scenery.

Even though it is the smallest and most urban Parroqui, the mountains and forests of Escaldes-Engordany have great ecological value: Vall del Madriu is an impressive itinery for hikers and one day it will be a Natural Park.

The ludic spa Caldea.

The church, on top of Turo d'Engolasters, is visible in all the Valley of Andorra la Vella and Escaldes-Engordany. Another well visited place in the Parroquia is the pre-Romanic church of Sant Miquel d'Engolaster, with only one nave, circular apse and square bell tower, covered by a tiled roof, added in the XII century. Close by, now in the Parroquia d'Encamp there is a placid glacial lake, surrounded by the only wood of Mediterranean Pines in Andorra where families go for picnics and to fish for trout. They hold an annual fishing contest.

A general view of Sant Juliá de Lória.

In the upper photo, the Germandat de Sant Juliá de Lória square.
Lower photo, the fountain in Laurédia square.

SANT JULIA DE LORIA

Touching the Spanish frontier it is the first Parroquia, agricultural and with tobacco factories, a product freely cultivated in Andorra. Twice a year, the fields on both sides of the road are filled with crops of this lush, perfumed plant with wide leaves and pink flowers.

The tobacco grown in Andorra is the black variety and in times of war "l'estraperlo", the Andorran cigar was well appreciated.

Bixessarri village.

Nowadays, this crop is fortunately protected by the State which obliges the manufacturers to buy all the production- some 400 tons - in exchange for manufacturing cigarettes under foreign licence (Marleboro, Stuyvesant, etc..).

The manufacturers only use a small part, the rest is burnt.

The Parroquia of Sant Juliá de Lloria is lowest in Andorra: the lowest point is where the rivers Runer and Valira join at 823m.

On this page several aspects of the fields of snow on the Rabassa, at 2,000m where mostly Nordic ski is practiced.

However, there are contrasts in height: the highest points are Pic del'Os or Bony de la Pica at 2,045m, the Port Negre at 2,665m and Pic de Monturull at 2,754. Sant Juliá de Lloria still conserves remains from the antique subdivision of the territory in Quarts.

Above, the Romanic church of Santa Filomena d'Aixovall and below, that of Sant Esteve de Bixessarri.

Above, the Romanic church of Sant Miquel de Fontaneda and below, a view from the church of Sant Pere d'Aixirivall.

Upper photo, a frontal view of the Canólic Sancturary
Below, the Romanic church of Sant Joan d'Aixás.

Many touristic routes lead to a dozen Romanic monuments scattered around the territory, and intimate villages with a clear Ibero -Basque toponomy, such as Juberri or Bixessarri. From this village it is possible to reach the hermitage of Mare de Déu de Canolich where, on the last Saturday of May, there is a gathering to venerate this Virgen. Many women in this Parroquia are called Canolich.

Above, the Romanic church of Sant Cerni de Nagol and below, the church of Sant Bartomeu in Sant Juliá.

On top of a cliff near to the road is the hermitage of Sant Cerni de Nagol, a magnificent example of Romanic architecture, the semi-circular apse with two splayed windows and sheer bell tower with double window. In 1980, fescos representing Cain and Abel, an eagle and a curious bearded Saint were discovered under a layer of lime.

Sant Antoni de la Grella church.

The Romanic bridge of Sant Antoni and the Massana tunnels.

LA MASSANA

On the confluence between the Valira del nord and Arinsal rivers, La Massana has the greatest number of summits in Andorra. Close to the road, on a level with the tunnels there is a sign which indicates the river banks, there is the bridge and church of Sant Antoni de la Grela, squating at the foot of the mountain. It was totally destroyed by the construction of the tunnels and rebuilt.

A wide and generous valley opens up on the other side of these tunnels, suroun

Upper, the church of Sant Cristófol d'Anyós
Below, Sispony village.

Upper photo, a view of the new buildings
and installations of Anyós's Sports Centre.
Beside, a view of the perfectly conserved
old quarter of Anyós

ded by peaks which are lit by reds, browns,
purples, yellows and oranges in the autumn.
The bottom of the valley narrows into a
gorge where the waters of a river flow, in
1982 this river brought mourning and
destruction.

Above, a general view of the Massana valley.
Below left, the church of Sant Iscle and Santa Victória de la Massana.
Right, a detail of the Massana.

The upper photo is a general view of La Massana
Above: tobacco leaves drying.
On the right a view of the village of l'Aldosa.

The upper photo is a general view of the village of Pal. On the left Sant Climent church in Pal and on the right a view of the village of Erts.

Like two separate twins the villages of Sispony and Anyos face each other across the valley. In this last village we find the beautiful XI century church of Sant Cristofol,

Upper right an aerial view of Arinsal and below right the Romanic church of Sant Andreu.

, which contains the remains of Romanic paintings, now in the USA and belonging to a private collection.

Other loved villages of this Parroquia, inhabited by a strong Anglophile community, are Erts, L'Aldosa, Pal and Arinsal. Two ski resorts have been installed beside these last two villages.

On the left a general view of the Ordino valley from the top of Ordino pass. In the background the mountains of Arcalis.
Upper right the church of Sant Corneli and Sant Cebrià.
Below a general view of Ordino.

ORDINO

The villages of Sornás, Ansalonga, LaCortinada have their own ancestral figure of administration, the Quart, separate from the Comu d'Ordino, while the hamlets of Segudet, Llorts, Arans and El Serrat depend on the capital of the Parroquia.

The Parroquia d'Ordino is the garden of Andorra as its inhabitants have conserved it, mantaining an archetectonic criteria at the same time as building modern establishments. The Pleta d'Ordino is a housing complex conceived by the country's architects.

Several aspects of the Areny-Plandolit museum in Ordino.

In the upper photo the beautiful village of Sornàs, On the right a view of Ansalonga and below cows pasturing in the fields of Ordino.

Upper left Cal Pal de la Cortinada, one of the oldest houses of Andorra. Below left a view of the Cortinada and above the church of Sant Martí de Cortinada.

The upper photo a global view of the Cortinada.
Below the restored mill and sawmill of can Pal in the Cortinada, XVI-XVII Century.

Above a view of Llorts and the Romanic church of Sant Cerni. On the left the Romanic bridge of Serrat.

Upper right: the numerous streams which fall as a cascade from the lakes of Tristaina.
Below right: the church of Sant Pere del Serrat.

In the XIX century the town of Ordino profited from its iron mines. The wrought iron balconies and doors of the well to do families are a sign of this industrial past. One of the most spectacular balconies is Casa Plandolit, which was the home of one of Andorra's noble families, d'Areny i Plandolit. Nowadays it is a museum.

Farther down the road after a tight curve there is a large Romanic church, Sant

On the left a view of the Vall d'Ordino from el Serrat. Below horses pasturing on Serrat. On the right the strong current of the Valira river in spring as it flows through the Ribera woods

Marti de la Cortinada, reconstructed throughout the centuries. However the undeniable interest of this church is its interior, with its relative well conserved paintings, discovered a few years ago, behind a wall constructed in the XVIII.

At the foot of the first house in Sornás, we can see prehistoric inscriptions.

Above: a retrospective view of the old Santuari de Meritxell 8th September, festival of the Virgin of Meritxell and National Day of Andorra..
Below right: present state of the old and restored Santuari de Meritxell, patron of the valleys of Andorra. On the page to the right a general view of the present complex of the Santuari de Meritxell, work of the architect Bofill.

CANILLO

The largest of the 7 Parroqies, (approx. 121 km2), and in ancient times the most important. The growth of the town of Andorra la Vella and Escaldes-Engordany has finished with the eminently rural Andorra of previous times, when the town of Canillo and the 12 hamlets - Incles, Els Plans, Ransolm L'Aldosa, El Vilar, El Forn, Prats, Molleres, Meritxell, El Tarter, Sant Pere del Tarter and Soldeu - scattered around its Parroquia lived from stockbreeding.

Above a view of the present Santuari de Meritxell. Below left: interior of the new sanctuary and on the right the carving of the Virgin of Meritxell a copy of the one which was lost in the fire,1972.

Above right a view of the arches
of the same Santuari de Meritxell
and below right the present aspect
of the interior of the old reformed
sanctuary

Nowadays the Parroqia of Canillo is known
essentially for its double ski resort Soldeu-El
Tarter, the beautiful Romanic church of Sant
Joan de Caselles and the sanctuary of
Meritxell.

    The chapel and the polychrome carving
of the Mare de Déu de Meritxell, patron of
the Valls d'Andorra the oldest in the Valls,
was destroyed in a fire, the night of the 8th-

Photo upper left: Cottages in Mantaup.
Above: an izard on the skirts of Canillo
Lower photo: the Montaup pass.

Two aspects of Canillo. Above a panoramic view in summer and below a winter view.

In the upper photo the
Romanic church of
of Sant Sant Joan de
Casselles one of the jewels
of Andorra
Below left,the witches rock
and on the right the
seven branched cross both
in Canillo.

Two aspects of the interior of the church of Sant Sant Joan de Casselles Above, the remains of Christ Majesty surrounded by frescos representing the sun and the moon above and the soldiers Longinus and Stefanon below.
The paintings and work in general belong to the XIIC
Below the altar piece of Sant Joan which represents different scenes from the life of Sant Joan, and his visions of the Apocalypse and the Passion of Christ. Dated XVI C.

On the other page on the left, a
nocturnal view of the church of
Sant Joan de Casselles, XII C. Above
the artificial wall for climbing in Canillo.
Above right a typical house in Tarter and
below two views of the Vall d'incles, one of the
most beautiful places in Andorra.

Above, a general view of Tarter from Ransol and below horses pasturing in Vall d'Incles.

On this page, a view of Soldeu and below a general view of El Tarter and Soldeu.

9th of September, 1972, after celebrating the National festival. In its place the famous Barcelona architect, Ricard Bofill has built a great sancturary. La Mare de Déu which is in the interior is a reproduction made by the Andorran sculptor Sergi Mas, before the fire.

The church of Sant Joan de Caselles near the road and beautifully illuminated at night - is a magnificent, well preserved example of Romanic architecture, basically from the XII century but with pieces from primitive Romanic and later constructions, such as the porch, XV century. In 1961, the pictures visible in the interior dated from XII century, were discovered.

Above a general view of Encamp and below
the Romanic church of Sant Romá de las Bons

ENCAMP

The central part of Andorra, a beautiful valley, closed by a circle of peaks of glacial origen, full of ponds and lakes: the Circ dels Pessons which arrives at the frontier with France where we find the village and ski resort of Pas de la Casa. The road which does not respect the ancestral division of territories passes through the Parroquia d'Encamp twice, crossing the Parroquia de Canillo through the middle as well as the undefined land called, paradoxically, by the name of Terreny de la Concordia (where we

Above left the church of Santa Eulalia. Above right the church of Sant Miquel de Mosquera Below left, the sports and social-cultural centre of Encamp and on the right the Casa Comuna of Encamp.

Above, aerial view of Englosters lake with Escades-Engordany and Andorra la Vella in the background.
Below horses pasturing in Envalira valley.
On the left page an impressive view of Els Cortals d'Encamp.

Above Pessons lake with Pic de Ribuls in the background.
Above left Montmalús pass., a curve of Envalira pass in winter, the step climb to
Envalira pass from Grau Roig, a aspect of Pas de la Casa, the road which joins Envalira
and Grau Roig and a general view of Pas de la Casa.

A lovely view of Pessons lake refuge in winter, completely covered with snow , below a view of Pessons covered in snow.

find the resort of Grau Roig, twin to Pas de la Casa), which the Parroquies of Canillo and d'Encamp have fought over for centuries.

The centre of the Parroquia includes the village of d'Encamp and the hamlets of La Mosquera, Les Bons, El Tremat, Vila, the lake of Engolasters and the magnificent scenery of Cortals d'Encamp. Romanic

A general view of Pas de la Casa in winter.

churches or chapels are scattered around the area: we must mention Sant Romá de les Bons, straight, proud on top of a spur which dominates the valley. It is pre-Romanic. Beside it are the remains of the Castle of the Moors. In the same village of Encamp, the parish church of Sant Eulália has the highest Romanic bell tower in Andorra. Partially Lombard in style. At the end of the '80's, it was the object of an important reform at the hand of the architects Mackay, Oriol Bohigas and Joan Martorell.

In summer a school of engraving, attracts many art students prinicipally from Barcelona.

Two contrasting aspects of Pas de la Casa. Above the village as it is now and below a retrospective view of the French customs and the frontier of Pas de la Casa in the post-war years.

Machines pressing the snow, and normal scene in the Andorran ski resorts
Below left, Soldeu after a snowfall.
On the right, a sledge pulled by dogs during a crossing of the Pyrenees.

A Sant Bernard watches the skiiers impassibly. On the right, a view of the snow covered woods of Soldeu.

SKI RESORTS

Andorra recieves 10 million visitors a year, essentially from Fance and Spain. The winter snow is one of the principal sources of the current Andorran prosperity and due to this at the beginning of the '80's the Andorran government declared the white gold national patrimony.

The 5 ski resorts (as well as a recently equiped one for cross country ski in Sant Julia de Loria, touching the frontier with Cataluyna), enjoy not only a constant thickness of snow but the Andorran resorts were the first in the Pyrenees to install snow cannons, they assure the first ski at Purisima and for the End of the Year, when snow is desired.

Moreover, Andorra has modern aprés-ski activities such as ice skating in the ice rink of Canillo and the Caldea spa sport and ludic complex, in Escaldes, unique in southern Europe.

Three different aspects of Arinsal ski resort.
Below right, a snowborder making a pirruette during a competition in Arinsal.

A view of the slopes of Pal, after a heavy snowfall.

ARINSAL AND PAL

The valley of La Massana has two ski resorts: Arinsal and Pal.

The resort of Arinsal, between 1,550 and 2,560 m high, has 28km of slopes: 2 green, 7 blue, 7 red and 5 black.

Arinsal has the novelty of a Half-Pipe slope for Snow-Board.

The resort of Pal, in the middle of a wood, is for family tourists who wish to ski on slopes with no difficulties.

There are 4 green, 3 blue, 12 red and one black. The circuit is 30 km.

Several aspects of Ordino-Arcalis ski resort.

ORDINO-ARCALIS

The resort of Ordino-Arcalis is placed in wild high, alp type mountain scenery. It is preferred by those who like difficult skiing and Snow-Board. It has very important changes in level and an important off slope ski. Among the new alternatives there is the heliski (ski from helicopter).

There are 24 km of slopes 6 green, 7 blue , 9 red and 2 black.

Above left, the cable car with Soldeu in the background. Below, a view of Soldeu village.
On the next page, above left, a view of the centre slope in Soldeu and below the new cable car. Above right, a view of Riba Escorch d'El Tarter refuge and below a panoramic view of Riba Escorchada d' El Tarter plateu.

SOLDEU-EL TARTER.

Soldeu-El Tarter is a double resort. It is very sunny and has a lot of snow and modern installations. Several night bars offer a very English atmosphere.

The two resorts together offer 60km of slopes: 11 green, 5 blue, 7 red and 6 black.

A view of Pas de la Casa ski resort. In close up the Costa Rodona refuge and in the background Coll Blanc.

PAS DE LA CASA-GRAU ROIG.

Certainly the best known and the most international resort. Next to the frontier, there is the French resort of Porté-Puymorens also a double resort, there is a project to connect them to Pas de la Casa which, facing north, is the only resort with an Atlantic orientation in the Principality of Andorra. Its twin resort Grau-Roig is orientated to the Mediterranean. Pas de la Casa-Grau Roig has a wide offer of slopes and is for the more experienced skiers who wish to experience strong emotions, while Grau-Roig, facing south, is very sunny and attracts a more family public. The alternatives are off slope skiing and night skiing. The town of Pas de la Casa is full of bars and discotheques with a good atmosphere and wide variety of music.

There are 85 km of slopes in Pas de la Casa-Grau-Roig, 13 green, 12 blue, 19 red and 8 black.

Above, a view of the four seater cablecar in
Pas de la Casa. Above right a general view
Pas de la Casa. Below a view of Grau Roig
resort and finally a view of Grau Roig with
the peak of Cubil in the background.

A curious retrospective view of the mail betwe Seu d'Urgell and Andorra la Vella 1938. Below smugglers from the same era arranging their packets.

CUSTUMS AND CURIOUS EVENTS.

Andorra is a country of traditions which neither foreigners, tourists nor the modernization of its institutions have been able to eliminate completely. Previous to the judicial and constitutional reform, Andorra's laws depended on Usos i Costums. These were collected, in the middle of the XVIII Century by Antoni Fiter i rossell in the Manual Digest and summarized in the Politar Andorrá by mossén Antoni Puig.

The last tradition to be modernized without being completely lost, is that of giving a red peseta to each voter in the Parroquia of Canillo. When the coin disappeared from the Spanish currency the community subisitutited it for a pin.

There is still the beautiful tradition of the Encantament dels Llibres. The people with debts to the Comu, have to pay them before a determined day during which time the messenger of the Comu stands in front of the door and proclaims...l'Encantament dels Llibres (of accounts), those who have not paid after this day will be fined with the Cot. those who have been notified of the Cot without result will pay the Recot. The Archive with the

original parchments of the Pareatges (founding document of the Co-principality of Andorra) can only be consulted in the presence of the 7 Consols (mayors-governers) of the 7 Parroqias of Andorra. Each of them has a key which they have to introduce simultaneously in the 7 keyholes. Nowadays, the achive is a safe. Until 1978, the documents were kept in the cupboard of 6 keys (as previous to creating the 7th

Two images
the live Nativity play
of Esteve Albert in
Escaldes
Engordany.

Parroquie, during 7 centuries there were only 6 Parroquias of Andorra). The cupboard of six keys was at the back of the room where the parliamentary sessions of the general Consell were held in the Casa de la Vall. Before the instigation of the new judicial institutions, when there was a violent death, the Batlle (judge) arrived and pronounced the traditional sentence: "Deadman, who killed you?" three times, before declaring: "He who does not answer is trully dead".

In 1936, a Russian called Boris, Baron of Skossyreff appeared in the Valls, he convinced the Sindic, maximum authority then elected, to make Andorra a monarchy. Boris 1, Prince of Andorra reigned for 6 days, until by order of the co-prince the Bishop, a squadron of Guardia Civil detained him. He had time though, to draft a Declaration of War against the Coprince-bishop. The Andorran writer Antioni Morell has published a version in novel of this episode in the history of Andorra.

Above left, a squirrel(Scirius Vlugaris) on a trunk in the wood. In middle a wild boar (Sus Scrofa).
On the right a weasel (Mustella Nivalis).

A pleasant image
of an izard
(Rupicara Pyrenaica)
near Sant
Joan de Casselles.

Above left, horses and
ponies pasturing.Centre left a
wild cock (Tetrao Urogallus),
Below left cows pasturing in
Cortals d'Encamp
Above right, , descending
Moles waterfall. Below right
mountain bike, canyoning on
the Valira and abseiling the
waterfall on d'Urina river.

"Grandalla"
(Narcisus Poeticus)

"Rapontic Pirenenc"
(Rhaponticum Centauroides)

"Minuartia Sedoide"
(Minuartia Sedoides)

"Manetes"
(Macrolepiota Procera)

Spring in the Valls

In ample representation
of Pyreneic flora headed
by the "Grandalla"
Andorra's national flower

"Abarset Neret"
(Rhododendrum
Ferrugineum)

Polinisation

"Saüc Racemós"
(Sambuscus Racemosa)

"Tora Blava"
(Aconitum Napellus)

"Epilobi Angustifoli"
(Epilobium Angustifolium)

"Flor de Pastor"
(Daphne Cneorum)

"Carlina"
(Carlina Cinara)

A beautiful image to leave with is this view of the Margineda bridge in autumn